MAGNET RECOGNITION PROGRAM®

TRANSFORMATIONAL LEADERSHIP 2023

ANCC
AMERICAN NURSES CREDENTIALING CENTER
MAGNET

AMERICAN NURSES CREDENTIALING CENTER MAGNET RECOGNITION PROGRAM®

The American Nurses Credentialing Center (ANCC) provides people and organizations in the nursing profession with the tools they need on their journey to excellence. ANCC recognizes healthcare organizations for nursing excellence through the Magnet Recognition Program®. ANCC is the largest and most prestigious nurse-credentialing organization in the United States.

Magnet® Program Office

The ANCC's Magnet Program Office staff manages and coordinates all aspects of the application and appraisal process.
Contact information is available at nursingworld.org/organizational-programs/magnet/contact-magnet-staff/.
For Magnet Recognition Program information online, visit: nursingworld.org/organizational-programs/magnet/
For Magnet Application Manual Updates and FAQs, visit: nursingworld.org/organizational-programs/magnet/magnet-manual-updates-and-faqs/

American Nurses Credentialing Center
A subsidiary of the American Nurses Association Enterprise
8515 Georgia Avenue, Suite 400
Silver Spring, MD 20910
ISBN-13:
Print: 978-1-953985-25-5
Epub: 978-1-953985-26-2
ePDF: 978-1-953985-27-9
Mobi: 978-1-953985-28-6

Disclaimers:

Please note this is an abridged version of the 2023 Magnet Recognition Program Application Manual. If your organization is considering pursuing ANCC Magnet Recognition®, the Magnet Application Manual is essential for understanding the full scope of application and documentation submission requirements. It is the only authorized publication that provides detailed information on the instructions and process for documentation submission.

Completing all the processes within the *Application Manual* facilitates Magnet recognition but does not, in and of itself, guarantee achievement.

Changes may be made by the ANCC to the Magnet Recognition Program and the *Application Manual* without notice. Applicants must confirm that they are using the most current edition of the *Application Manual* before preparing written documentation for submission to the ANCC Magnet Program Office. For application information and *Application Manual* updates, go to www.nursingworld.org/organizational-programs/magnet/.

The Magnet Recognition Program® Mission and Vision

Mission: The Magnet Recognition Program® will continually elevate patient care around the world in an environment where nurses, in collaboration with the interprofessional team, flourish by setting the standard for excellence through leadership, scientific discovery, and dissemination and implementation of new knowledge.

Vision: The Magnet Recognition Program will transform healthcare globally by bringing knowledge, skill, innovation, leadership, and compassion to every person, family, and community.

—Commission on Magnet, 2020

Contents

Preface

The American Nurses Credentialing Center (ANCC) and the Commission on Magnet (COM) are pleased to present the 2023 Magnet® Application Manual. This updated version (13th Edition) contains current information and instructions to guide Magnet® designated organizations as well as those considering the Journey to Magnet Excellence®.

ANCC Magnet designation is the highest credential a healthcare organization can achieve. It acknowledges the invaluable contributions of nurses in all healthcare settings and among all populations around the world. Magnet designation is an indication to patients and the public that these organizations have met the most stringent, evidence-based standards of nursing excellence in patient care delivery. It is a results-driven recognition that fosters nurse engagement, and the role nurses play as members of the interprofessional team to improve patient outcomes and reduce healthcare costs.

The revisions to the 2023 Magnet® Application Manual reflect evidence spanning 34 years of research and development. These revisions are driven by the improvements and progress seen in healthcare delivery systems around the world. The 2023 Manual was developed with input from subject matter experts including members of the Commission on Magnet, Magnet Program Office, and feedback from the field. Changes to the 2023 Manual clarify previous standards, acknowledge the importance of diversity of healthcare workers and patients, and expand upon standards in the context of an ever-evolving ambulatory care environment.

The Magnet Recognition Program's 2023 Mission and Vision inspire a sustained focus on patient care in interprofessional healthcare settings of excellence. The 2023 Magnet Application Manual standards continue to raise the bar for nursing with the ongoing development of new nursing knowledge and integration of evidence-based nursing practice. The value nurses bring to patient care, healthcare organizations, their communities, and the world is undeniable. Magnet designated organizations—of every size, patient-delivery setting, and in any location—examine and communicate a scientific impact on exemplary care delivery outcomes in the 21st century and beyond.

Jeanette Ives Erickson, DNP, RN, NEA-BC, FAAN
Chair, Commission on Magnet

Rebecca Graystone, MS, MBA, RN, NE-BC
Vice President, ANCC Magnet Recognition Program

Chapter 1

THE MAGNET® MODEL

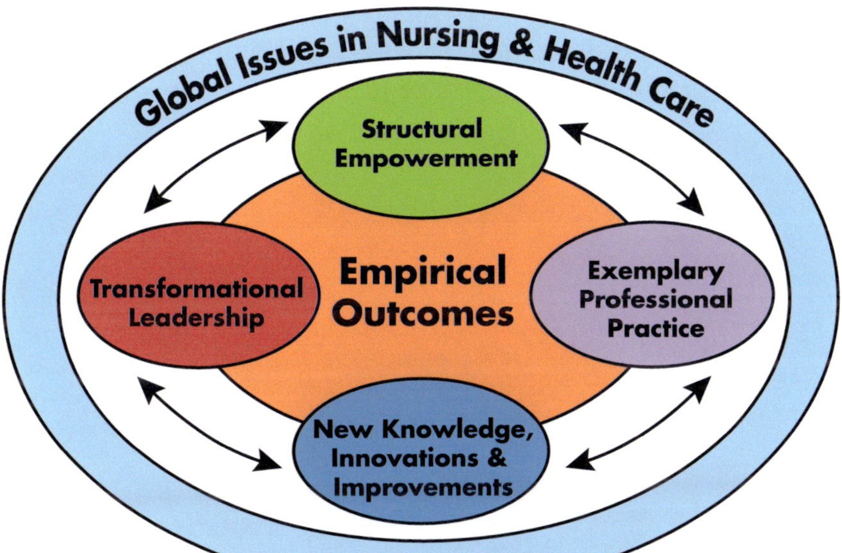

The Forces of Magnetism that were identified more than forty years ago have remained remarkably stable—a testament to their enduring value. The Magnet Recognition Program® evolved over time in response to changes in the healthcare environment.

Statistical Foundation: The Empirical Model

In 2007, the American Nurses Credentialing Center (ANCC) commissioned a statistical analysis of final appraisal scores for applicants under the *2005 Magnet Recognition Program Application Manual* (ANCC 2004). The project goal was to examine the relationships among the Forces of Magnetism by investigating alternative frameworks for structuring the Source of Evidence (SOE) examples and to inform development of the new Magnet Model. The newly developed Magnet Model first presented in the *2008 Magnet Recognition Program Application Manual* provided a new perspective on the SOE examples and how they combine to create a work environment that supports excellence in nursing (Figure 1.1).

Figure 1.1. Triaxial Diagram

Through a combination of factor analysis, cluster analysis, and multidimensional scaling, the final SOE example scores were examined to determine how they might be organized based solely on their empirical properties. The results suggested an alternative framework for grouping the SOE examples. The empirical model yielded from this analysis informed the conceptual development of the current Magnet Model. Over the years, each subsequent manual has used a rigorous process, resulting in Magnet organizations creating a continued culture of excellence and innovation in nursing.

Excellence is determined through the evaluation of SOE examples, which demonstrate the infrastructure for excellence. The examples, provided by Magnet organizations, incorporate narratives to describe the structure and process used to achieve improved outcomes. These narratives demonstrate how the structures and processes are present and operationalized within the organization.

Before the *2019 Magnet Application Manual* was published, the Magnet Program Office (MPO) conducted an extensive evaluation of the characteristics of documentation submitted for review that met the threshold to move to the Site Visit Phase. The results indicated organizations that consistently demonstrated the development, dissemination, and enculturation of the Magnet Model Components in their documentation were the most successful. This finding established the expectation—for Initial Applicants and Magnet designated organizations alike—that the SOE example narratives and supporting evidence presented in an organization's documentation reflect enculturation of Magnet Component SOE requirements in their entirety across the depth and breadth of the organization, wherever nursing is practiced.

The 2023 Magnet Application Manual embraces the foundation set by the original study and ensuing Magnet manuals while acknowledging the importance of diversity, equity, inclusion and well-being of healthcare workers, patients, and communities; expands upon standards in the context of an ever-evolving ambulatory care environment; and raises the bar for nursing with the ongoing development of new nursing knowledge and the integration of evidence-based nursing practice.

Section II

EMPIRICAL OUTCOMES (EO) COMPONENT

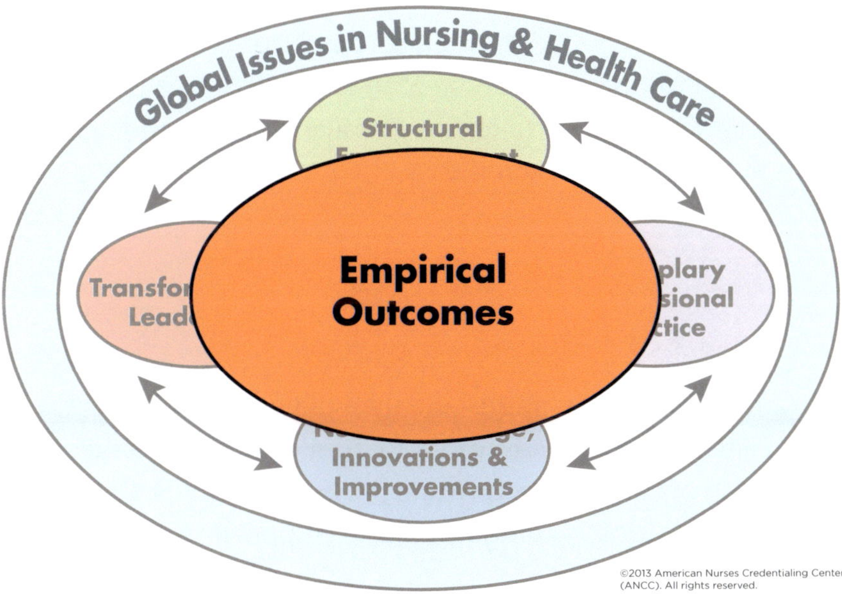

Professional nursing makes essential contributions to patient care, nursing workforce, organizational, healthcare, and consumer outcomes. The empirical measurement of quality outcomes related to nursing leadership and clinical practice in Magnet designated organizations is imperative. The 2008 introduction of the Magnet Model to incorporate outcomes represented a fundamental shift for the Magnet Recognition Program with the addition of the third component of Donabedian's Model of Quality—structure, process, and outcome. Previous Magnet Application Manuals emphasized structure and process and, although structure and process create the infrastructure for excellence in Magnet designated healthcare organizations, the impact of that infrastructure—outcomes—is essential to a culture of excellence and innovation. Outcomes demonstrate the achievement of desired results that are based on the healthcare team's application of sound structure and processes that exist within the organization and its systems of care.

Required Empirical Outcome (EO) Source of Evidence (SOE) examples are integrated throughout the Magnet Model Components in this Application Manual. Section II establishes the requirements for formatting narratives, graphs, and data tables, for the EO SOE examples.

Empirical Outcome (EO) SOE Examples: Presentation Requirements

Displaying data using graphs and data tables is an excellent way to illustrate outcomes resulting from the healthcare team's application of sound structure and process measures; therefore, a graph with corresponding data table (supporting evidence) is required for each EO SOE.

There are **unique EO SOE examples** that are identified in the bulleted list below that must be presented in specific formats. Specific presentation requirements for these unique examples are depicted within their respective EO SOE examples and located in the 2023 Magnet Application Manual on the page number(s) noted below.

- Page 40: Professional board certification (SE4EO)
- Page 41: Professional board certification (SE6EO)
- Page 45: Nursing education (SE8EO)
- Page 57: Registered nurse satisfaction/registered nurse engagement (EP3EO)
- Page 65: Nurse turnover rate (EP12EO)
- Page 69: Nurse-sensitive clinical quality indicators (EP19EO)
- Page 71: Nurse-sensitive clinical quality indicators (EP20EO)
- Page 74: Patient experience (EP21EO)
- Page 77: Patient experience (EP22EO)

All other EO SOE examples must be presented using the following Empirical Outcomes Presentation Requirements:

When using the empirical outcomes format, the example provided must have occurred within the 48 months prior to documentation submission.

PROBLEM

Describe the identified problem that exist(s) in the applicant organization that you worked to improve.

NOTE:* The problem, pre-intervention(s), goal, intervention(s), and outcome must align.

Analysts' tip: The outcome data drive the problem statement.

PRE-INTERVENTION

Describe the pre-intervention outcome data that drove the goal and initiative (must have occurred within the 48 months prior to documentation submission).

Describe the actions/activities that took place prior to the implementation of the intervention(s).

Include the timeline of dates of the actions/activities and the names of the key individual(s) involved.

GOAL STATEMENT

Provide the goal statement.

Include the outcome measure that aligns with the goal to demonstrate the improvement(s).

Include the location of the desired improvement.

Analysts' tip: The stated goal *must* align with the graphed outcome data.

* *Information in NOTES is very important as it conveys a requirement and/or directive.*

PARTICIPANTS

- List participants involved in the pre-intervention and intervention activities or initiative.
- Include name, discipline, job title, and department.

INTERVENTION

- Describe the actions/activities that took place to facilitate the change and that had an impact on the problem to result in the achievement of the improvement/outcome.
- Include the timeline of dates of the actions/activities and the names of the key individual(s) involved.
- Include where and when the intervention(s) occurred (e.g., unit, department, service line, organization).
- Include a description of how the intervention(s) impacted the outcome.
- Provide key references (minimum of two) to support the interventions were evidence-based.

> NOTE: American Psychological Association (APA) format should be followed.

OUTCOME

- Provide trended data (i.e., a minimum of one pre-intervention data point and three post-intervention data points) demonstrating an improved trend.

- Pre-intervention and post-intervention data must be displayed to indicate the impact of an intervention or series of interventions on the outcome.
- The trended data must be displayed as a graph and table with data elements clearly provided.

NOTE: The data point immediately prior to the intervention period cannot be zero.

Analysts' tip: See glossary for the full definition of *outcome*.

DATA DISPLAY REQUIREMENTS

- The graph must include dates, location of data collection, legend, and title.
- Indicate on the graph the pre-intervention, intervention, and post-intervention timeframes.
- The *x*-axis units-of-time must be the same for pre-intervention and post-intervention data (e.g., quarters, months).
- The *y*-axis units of measure represent the desired outcome. Data must be presented as ratio (e.g., rates, percentiles, percentages). Additionally, the data must be consistent throughout the data collection period.
- If data are presented for a fiscal year, the period defining the fiscal year must be defined with calendar year equivalent (January to December and year; June to May and year).

- Pre-Intervention and Post-Intervention timelines must be consecutive and consistent (e.g., days to days, months to months, quarters to quarters, etc.) or time intervals that are consistent with established *performance improvement methodologies*.

- The Pre-Intervention, Intervention, and Post-Intervention periods may not intersect.

Analysts' tip: Align the timelines in the narrative and the improvements (outcomes) displayed on the graph.

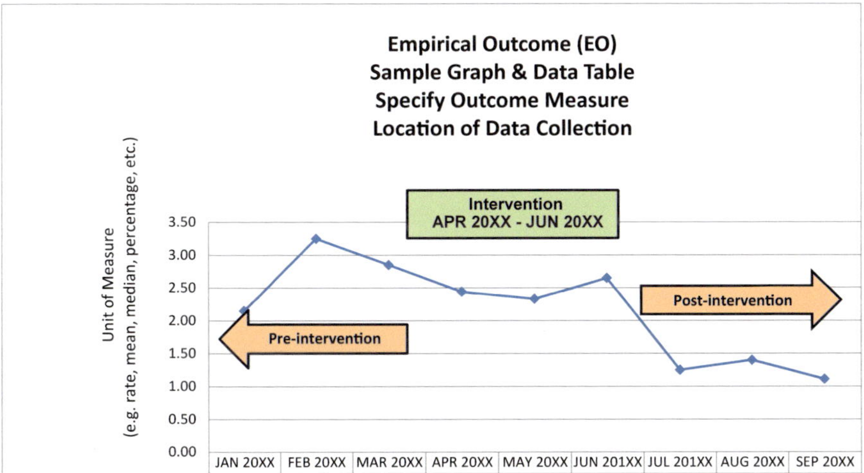

	JAN 20XX	FEB 20XX	MAR 20XX	APR 20XX	MAY 20XX	JUN 201XX	JUL 201XX	AUG 20XX	SEP 20XX
Outcome measure	2.15	3.25	2.85	2.44	2.33	2.65	1.25	1.40	1.11

Figure II.1. Empirical Outcomes (EO) Sample Graph and Data Table

Section III

TRANSFORMATIONAL LEADERSHIP (TL) COMPONENT

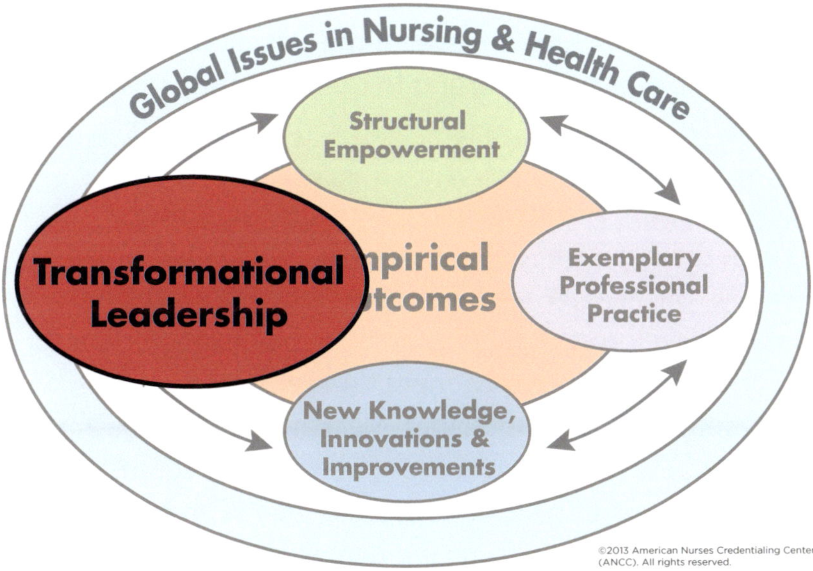

The Chief Nursing Officer (CNO) in a Magnet® designated organization is a knowledgeable, transformational leader who develops a strong vision and well-articulated philosophy, a professional practice model*, and strategic and quality plans in leading nursing services.

* *This formatting indicates that these words and phrases are defined in the Glossary. Please refer to the Glossary for full explanations of these terms.*

The transformational CNO communicates expectations, develops leaders, and evolves the organization to meet current and anticipated needs and strategic priorities. Nursing leaders at all levels of the organization demonstrate advocacy and support on behalf of staff and patients.

The CNO must be strategically positioned within the organization to effectively influence other executive stakeholders, including the board of directors or board of trustees. Strategic positioning is imperative to lead and influence others, both operationally and during periods of change management due to internal or external factors. Executive-level nursing leaders serve at the highest level of the organization, with the CNO typically reporting to the Chief Executive Officer (CEO).

Nursing's mission, vision, values, and strategic plan must align with the organization's priorities to improve the organization's performance. Wherever nursing is practiced, the CNO must develop structures, processes, and expectations for clinical nurse input and involvement throughout the organization to effect desired outcomes. Mechanisms must be implemented for evidence-based practice to evolve and for innovation to flourish. The CNO should be seen as an executive leader and a nursing advocate and perceived as leading nursing practice and patient care. The CNO should be visible and accessible and should communicate effectively in an environment of mutual respect and inclusion. As a result, nurses throughout the organization should perceive that their diverse voices are heard, their input is valued, and their practice and professional well-being are supported.

The intent of the Transformational Leadership component is to reflect the following:

- Nursing's mission, vision, values, and strategic plan align with the organization's priorities to improve performance.
- Nurses advocate for resources to support nursing unit and organizational goals.
- The CNO influences organization-wide change beyond the scope of nursing.
- The CNO is a strategic partner in the organization's decision-making.
- Nurse leaders lead effectively through change.
- The CNO advocates for organizational support of ongoing leadership development for all nurses, with a focus on mentoring and succession planning.
- Executive nurse leaders and Nurse Managers, with clinical nurse input, use trended data to acquire necessary resources to support the care delivery system(s) and clinician well-being.
- The CNO uses various methods to communicate, be visible, and be accessible to nurses throughout the organization.
- Executive nurse leaders use input from clinical nurses to influence change in the organization.

Organizational Overview

The Organizational Overview (OO) items contain requests for documents and information that are foundational to Magnet® designated organizations and provide background information that informs the Magnet® Appraisers about the enculturation of the Magnet Components throughout the organization.

Transformational Leadership

OO3

Provide:

- The current Chief Nursing Officer's (CNO) job description;
- CNO's curriculum vitae or resume;
- The organization chart(s);
- The nursing organization chart(s);
- A description of the CNO's structural and operational relationships to all areas in which nursing is practiced; and
- Names and credentials, of all individuals serving as the CNO, in the 48 months preceding document submission. Include the tenure dates.

STRATEGIC PLANNING

TL1

Provide one example, with supporting evidence, of an initiative in nursing practice that is consistent with the organization's mission statement.

- Provide a copy of the organization's mission statement as one of the supporting documents.

TL2

Provide one example, with supporting evidence, of a Nurse Assistant Vice President's (AVP's)/Nurse Director's or Nurse Manager's participation in an initiative which promoted workplace diversity, equity, and/or inclusion and is consistent with the organization's strategic plan.

- Provide a copy of the related organization's strategic plan.

Analysts' tip: The example provided can pertain to either the workforce, patients, or families.

TL3EO

Using the required empirical outcomes (EO) presentation format, provide one example of an improved patient outcome that aligns with a goal in the nursing strategic plan.

- Provide a copy of the related nursing strategic plan.

NOTE:* The nursing strategic plan may be part of the organization's strategic plan. If this is the case, the presence of nursing information in the strategic plan must be evident.

ADVOCACY AND INFLUENCE

TL4

a. Provide one example, with supporting evidence, of a Nurse AVP's/Nurse Director's advocacy for resources to support an organizational goal.

   AND

b. Provide one example, with supporting evidence, of a Nurse Manager's advocacy for resources to support a unit goal.

TL5

a. Provide one example, with supporting evidence, of the CNO's advocacy for and acquisition of organizational resources specific to nurses' well-being.

   AND

b. Provide one example, with supporting evidence, of a nurse's(s') (exclusive of the CNO) advocacy for and acquisition of resources specific to nurses' well-being at the unit or department/division level.

---

* *Information in NOTES is very important as it conveys a requirement and/or directive.*

For both TL5 examples, one of the following five elements must be incorporated:

- Work-Life Balance
- Health and Safety
- Employee Growth and Development
- Employee Recognition
- Employee Involvement

Analysts' tip: See glossary for the definitions of *well-being* and each of the five elements listed above.

TL6

Provide one example, with supporting evidence, of the CNO's leadership that led to a strategic organizational change beyond the scope of nursing.

NOTE: Organizational change must be inclusive of nursing and other departments.

TL7

Provide one example, with supporting evidence, of a Nurse AVP/ Nurse Director's or Nurse Manager's leadership that successfully guided nurses through change.

TL8EO

Using the required empirical outcomes (EO) presentation format, provide one example of an improved patient outcome, associated with a Nurse AVP's/Nurse Director's or Nurse Manager's membership in an organization-level, decision-making group.

- Patient outcome data may be presented at the organizational, division, or unit level.

VISIBILITY, ACCESSIBILITY, AND COMMUNICATION

TL9

Choose two of the following (one example must be from the ambulatory care setting, if applicable):

NOTE: If an organization has no ambulatory areas, then two inpatient examples must be provided

a. Provide one example, with supporting evidence, of an individual mentoring plan or an established mentoring program for a clinical nurse(s).

NOTE: The mentor for the clinical nurse must be a nurse.

b. Provide one example, with supporting evidence, of an individual mentoring plan or an established mentoring program for a Nurse Manager(s).

NOTE: The mentor for the Nurse Manager role must be a nurse.

c. Provide one example, with supporting evidence, of an individual mentoring plan or an established mentoring program for a Nurse AVP(s)/Nurse Director(s).

NOTE: The mentor for the Nurse AVP/Nurse Director role must be a nurse.

d. Provide one example, with supporting evidence, of an individual mentoring plan or an established mentoring program for an APRN(s).

NOTE: The mentor for the APRN role must be a nurse.

e. Provide one example, with supporting evidence, of an individual mentoring plan or an established mentoring program for the CNO.

Analysts' tip: The mentor to the CNO is not required to be a nurse.

TL10

Choose two of the following (one example must be from the ambulatory care setting, if applicable):

NOTE: If an organization has no ambulatory areas, then two inpatient examples must be provided.

a. Provide one example, with supporting evidence, of succession-planning activities for the Nurse Manager role.

b. Provide one example, with supporting evidence, of succession-planning activities for the Nurse AVP/Nurse Director role.

c. Provide one example, with supporting evidence, of succession-planning activities for the APRN role.

d. Provide one example, with supporting evidence, of succession-planning activities for the CNO role.

TL11EO

Using the required empirical outcomes (EO) presentation format, provide one example of an improved outcome where a clinical nurse(s) used data to advocate for the acquisition of a resource, in support of the care delivery system(s).

TL12

Provide an example, with supporting evidence, of a nurse's(s') advocacy for individual or community health promotion at an external forum where decisions impacting healthcare are made.

Analysts' tips:

- An external forum may be a government or non-government organization which can influence the nursing profession and/or the overall health of individuals or the community.
- See glossary for the definition of *health promotion*.

TL13EO

NOTE: If an organization has no ambulatory areas, then two inpatient examples must be provided.

Choose two of the following (one example must be from the ambulatory care setting, if applicable):

a. Using the required empirical outcomes (EO) presentation format, provide one example of an improvement in patient care or the nursing practice environment, associated with communication between the clinical nurse(s) and the CNO.

Analysts' tip: Communication can be either direct or indirect.

b. Using the required empirical outcomes (EO) presentation format, provide one example of an improvement in patient care or the nursing practice environment, associated with communication between the clinical nurse(s) and the Nurse AVP/Nurse Director.

Analysts' tip: Communication can be either direct or indirect.

c. Using the required empirical outcomes (EO) presentation format, provide one example of an improvement in patient care or the nurse practice environment, associated with communication between the clinical nurse(s) and a Nurse Manager.

Analysts' tip: Communication can be either direct or indirect.

Appendix D

SOURCE OF EVIDENCE (SOE) EXAMPLES—TYPES AND WRITING GUIDANCE

The *2023 Magnet® Application Manual* requirements are organized by Magnet Model Components, which require two general types of formatting and supporting evidence as depicted below. The Source of Evidence (SOE) examples provided in the documentation submitted by the organization should depict the Magnet characteristics embedded in and enculturated throughout the organization. Each SOE example must be clearly identified and requires a separate narrative. Descriptions of processes or programs must be accompanied by examples to illustrate how each is operationalized within the organization. The written documentation should provide examples from different departments or units to represent a variety of specialties and nursing leadership in the organization. The goal of the narratives is to clearly illustrate how the examples depict a dynamic and innovative focus on excellence as well as how they are integrated and enculturated across the organization.

Information offered for additional clarity and/or direction throughout the Magnet Application Manual is highlighted as follows:

Analysts' tip: information provided to serve as guidance

NOTE:* information that conveys a requirement and/or directive

Empirical Outcome (EO) SOE Examples

The EO SOE example narrative and supporting evidence must include:

- Problem
    - The identified problem that exist(s) in the applicant organization.
    - The problem, pre-intervention(s), goal, intervention(s), and outcome must align.
    - The outcome data drive the problem statement.
- Pre-Intervention
    - The pre-intervention outcome data that drove the goal and initiative
    - The actions/activities that took place prior to the implementation of the intervention(s)
    - The timeline of dates of the actions/activities
    - The names of the individual(s) involved
- Goal statement
    - The outcome measure that aligns with the goal to demonstrate the improvement(s).

* *Information in NOTES is very important as it conveys a requirement and/or directive.*

    - The location
    - Alignment with the graphed outcome data
- Participants
    - List of participants involved in the pre-intervention and intervention activities or initiative.
    - Name, discipline, job title, and department.
    - A meeting sign-in sheet is not required in addition to the participant list in an EO SOE example.
- Intervention
    - Description of the actions/activities that took place to facilitate the change and that had an impact on the problem to result in the achievement of the improvement/outcome.
    - The timeline of dates of the actions/activities and the names of the key individual(s) involved.
    - Where and when the intervention(s) occurred (e.g., unit, department, product line, organization).
    - How the intervention(s) impacted the outcome.
    - Provide key references (minimum of two) to support the interventions were evidence-based. Note: American Psychological Association (APA) format should be followed.
- Outcome

- Trended data (i.e., a minimum of one pre-intervention data point and three post-intervention data points) demonstrating an improved trend.
- Pre-intervention and post-intervention data must be displayed to indicate the impact of an intervention or series of interventions on the outcome.
- The trended data must be displayed as a graph and table with data elements clearly provided.

- Data display requirements are also found in the 2023 Magnet Application Manual, Chapter 3, page 26.

IMPORTANT: All examples and supporting evidence must have occurred within the 48 months prior to documentation submission. This requirement includes data presentation See Appendix C Timelines for exceptions to this requirement.

- The graphed outcome data, presented to substantiate the example narrative, represent the supporting evidence.
- Align the timelines in the narrative with the data displayed on the graph.
- Outcome data must be presented as a ratio (e.g., rate, percentage, average, mean, median) consistently throughout the data collection period. The only exception is with a "sentinel" or "never" event.
- A limited number of EO SOE examples require specific supporting documentation. This will be depicted in the example.
- Redact all protected health information (PHI).

Unique EO SOE Example presentations are required and depicted within the respective EO SOE examples in the 2023 Magnet Application Manual:

- Page 40: Professional board certification (SE4EO)
- Page 41: Professional board certification (SE6EO)
- Page 45: Nursing education (SE8EO)
- Page 57: Registered nurse satisfaction/registered nurse engagement (EP3EO)
- Page 65: Nurse turnover rate (EP12EO)
- Page 69: Nurse-sensitive clinical quality indicators (EP19EO)
- Page 71: Nurse-sensitive clinical quality indicators (EP20EO)
- Page 74: Patient engagement (EP21EO)
- Page 77: Patient engagement (EP22EO)

Inpatient vs. ambulatory setting examples:

- If two examples are requested (one ambulatory/one inpatient) and ambulatory settings do not exist in the organization, then two inpatient setting examples must be provided.
- If the EO SOE example request is not specific regarding the inpatient or ambulatory care setting, the example may be written about either setting.
- Ambulatory organizations that do not have any inpatient settings provide only ambulatory examples.

- Ambulatory examples must be specific to the ambulatory setting; all data must be from the ambulatory setting as well.
- Benchmarked data specific only to ambulatory units/areas: if a quarterly benchmark is not available, provide the available reporting timeframe (e.g., monthly, annual) to represent the equivalent of eight quarters of benchmarked data.

Source of Evidence (SOE) Examples Not Requiring Empirical Outcome (EO) Data [also referred to as a "Non-Empirical SOE example"]

The non-EO SOE examples and supporting evidence must occur within the 48-month period prior to the submission of written documentation. All protected health information (PHI) must be redacted before documentation submission.

The non-EO SOE example is written as follows:

- Narrative Statement: A description that concisely conveys how the key elements of the SOE example statement are present and operationalized within the organization. The Narrative Statement:
    - Must be a straightforward and concise description of how the SOE example is present and operationalized within the organization.
    - Must address the key words and phrases (key elements) in the SOE request statement.
    - Organizations with flat organizational structures, such as without Nurse Managers: the Nurse AVP/Nurse Director may be substituted for Nurse Manager SOE example(s).

- Example must have occurred within the 48 months prior to documentation submission.

IMPORTANT: The use of the EO SOE example outline template should not be used when writing non-EO SOE examples.

- Supporting evidence:
  - Comprised of item(s) that support and substantiate what is stated in the narrative statements which must have occurred within the 48 months prior to documentation submission.
  - Verifies that what is stated in the narrative exists in the organization.
  - Must substantiate narrative that addresses the key words and phrases (key elements) in the SOE request statement.
  - Limit of five supporting evidence items per non-EO SOE example.
  - Acceptable supporting evidence includes (but is not limited to):
    - Copies of written policies and procedures, files, intranet sites, meeting minutes, various types of correspondence, data, rosters, committee charters, job descriptions, and screenshots.
  - To be valid, supporting evidence must:
    - Be dated;
    - Contain signatures (as applicable);
    - Be legible; and

    - Include participants described in the example (e.g., name, position, title), as applicable.
- Supporting evidence does not include:
    - Photographs;
    - Testimonial statements; and
    - Documents generated for the purpose of clarifying the narrative.

Inpatient vs. ambulatory setting examples:

- If the SOE example request is not specific regarding the inpatient or ambulatory care setting, the example may be written about either setting.

- If two examples are requested (one ambulatory/one inpatient) and the organization does not include ambulatory settings, then two inpatient setting examples must be provided. Ambulatory organizations that do not have any inpatient settings provide only ambulatory examples.

- SOE examples that request narrative specific to ambulatory areas must be specific to the ambulatory setting. The narrative cannot take place in both inpatient and ambulatory areas.

Analysts' tip: The Magnet Program Office strongly recommends participation in the webinar Preparing a Successful Document—Critical Information. This webinar is available to applicants or members of the Magnet Learning Communities. Data indicate there is a corresponding increased success rate for organizations that view the webinar. For information, contact your regional Magnet Program Specialist (MPS).

Glossary for TL Component

care delivery system

A system for the delivery of care that delineates the nurses' authority and accountability for clinical decision-making and outcomes. "The care delivery system is integrated with the professional practice model and promotes continuous, consistent, efficient, and accountable delivery of nursing care. The care delivery system is adapted to meet evidence-based practice standards, national patient safety goals, affordable and value-based outcomes, and regulatory requirements. It describes the manner in which care is delivered, the skill set required, the context of care, and the expected outcomes of care" (American Nurses Credentialing Center, 2013, pp. 41–42).

clinical nurse

For Magnet purposes, the registered nurse who spends the majority (□51%) of their time providing direct patient care, including APRNs, who spend the majority of their time providing direct patient care.

employee growth and development

"Focuses on issues related to improving employee competencies and career development" (Grawitch & Ballard, 2016).

employee involvement

"Focuses on providing employees with a greater level of autonomy in their work as well as opportunities to be involved in organizational decision making" (Grawitch & Ballard, 2016).

employee recognition

"Focuses on demonstrating appreciation for employee contributions and includes both monetary and nonmonetary rewards" (Grawitch & Ballard, 2016).

evidence-based practice

"A problem-solving approach to clinical decision making within a health-care organization. It integrates the best available scientific evidence with the best available experiential (patient and practitioner) evidence. EBP [evidence-based practice] considers internal and external influences on practice and encourages critical thinking in the judicious application of such evidence to care of the individual patient, patient population, or system" (Dearholt & Dang, 2012).

health and safety

"Focuses on prevention, assessment, and treatment of potential health risks and problems and encouraging and supporting healthy lifestyle and behavior choices" (Grawitch & Ballard, 2016).

health promotion

"Covers a wide range of social and environmental interventions that are designed to benefit and protect individual people's health and quality of life by addressing and preventing the root causes of ill health, not just focusing on treatment and cure." The three key elements of health promotion are good governance for health, health literacy, and health cities (World Health Organization, 2016).

influence

"Actions that either directly or indirectly cause a change in the behavior and/or attitudes of another individual or group. The primary effect of leadership" (Shortell & Kaluzny, 2006, p. 533).

mentor

"An experienced nurse who has developed expertise and can be a strong force in shaping a nurse's identity as a professional" (Anthony, 2006, p. 73). Mentoring can include providing information, advice, support, and ideas. Typically, mentors and mentees have a long-lasting relationship. The terms "mentor" and "preceptor" are not used interchangeably.

mission

A statement of the good or benefit the healthcare organization intends to contribute, couched in terms of an identified community, a set of services, and a specific level of cost or finance (Griffith & White, 2002, p. 679).

Nurse Assistant Vice President (AVP)

Registered nurses with line authority over multiple units who have registered nurses working to deliver nursing care in an inpatient or ambulatory care setting and are positioned on the organizational chart between the Nurse Manager and the Chief Nursing Officer. This may include registered nurses who may broadly influence or impact the clinical practice of nurses in the organization. If these nurses are referenced as AVP in the organization's Magnet® documentation, they must meet the educational criteria (bachelor's in nursing or higher) and report directly or indirectly to the CNO. Examples may include nurse AVPs responsible for, but not limited to, nurse educators, registered nurse director of risk management or quality, registered nurse director of nursing informatics, infection preventionists, and wound ostomy nurses. The title "AVP" reflects the function of the role for the purpose of documentation submission. It is understood that registered nurses who function in an AVP role in the organization may not be assigned the title "AVP."

Nurse Director

Registered nurses with line authority over multiple units that have registered nurses working to deliver nursing care in an inpatient or ambulatory care setting and are positioned on the organizational chart between the Nurse Manager and the Chief Nursing Officer. This may include registered nurses who may broadly influence or impact the clinical practice of nurses in the organization. If these nurses are referenced as a director in the organization's Magnet® documentation, they must meet the educational criteria (bachelor's in nursing or higher) and report directly or indirectly to the CNO. Examples may include directors responsible for, but not limited to, nurse educators, RN director of risk management or quality, RN director of nursing informatics, infection preventionists, and wound ostomy nurses. The title "director" reflects the function of the role for the purpose of documentation submission. It is understood that registered nurses who function in a director role in the organization may not be assigned the title of director.

Nurse Manager

Registered nurses with the accountability and supervision of all registered nurses and other healthcare providers who deliver nursing care in an inpatient or ambulatory care setting. The Nurse Manager is typically responsible for recruitment and retention, performance review, and professional development; is involved in the budget formulation process and quality outcomes; and helps plan for, organize, and lead the delivery of nursing care for a designated patient care area. The title "Nurse Manager" reflects the function of the role for the purpose of documentation submission. It is understood that registered nurses who function in a Nurse Manager role in the organization may not be assigned the title of Nurse Manager.

nurse practice environment

"The organizational characteristics of a work setting that facilitate or constrain professional nursing practice." It is a complex construct with theoretical foundations in the sociology of organizations, occupations, and work. The nursing professional practice environment reveals an organization's approach to resolving the dilemmas of "how to organize many workers to perform a large-scale task; how to organize professional staff; and how to organize work that is inherently complex and unpredictable" (Lake, 2002, pp. 177–178).

nursing practice environment

See *nurse practice environment*.

performance

Achievement of a desired result (Shortell & Kaluzny, 2006, p. 538).

professional practice model

"It is a schematic description of a system, theory, or phenomenon that depicts how nurses practice, collaborate, communicate, and develop professionally to provide the highest-quality care for those served by the organization (e.g., patients, families, communities)" (Silverstein & Kowalski, 2017). Professional practice models illustrate "the alignment and integration of nursing practice with the mission, vision, and values that nursing has adopted" (American Nurses Credentialing Center, 2013).

scope of nursing practice

"The description of the *who, what, where, when, why,* and *how* of nursing practice that addresses the range of nursing practice activities common to all registered nurses. When considered in conjunction with the Standards of Professional Nursing Practice and the Code of Ethics for Nurses, comprehensively describes the competent level of nursing common to all registered nurses" (American Nurses Association, 2021).

strategic plan

A plan resulting from a process of "reviewing the mission, environmental surveillance, and previous planning decisions used to establish major goals and nonrecurring resource allocation decisions" (Griffith & White, 2002, p. 683).

succession planning

"A strategic process involving identification, development, and evaluation of intellectual capital, ensuring leadership continuity within an organization" (Titzer & Shirey, 2013, p. 158).

values

An expansion of the mission that expresses basic rules of acceptable conduct, such as respect for human dignity or acceptance of equality (Griffith & White, 2002, p. 684).

well-being

Professional well-being is a function of being satisfied with one's job, finding meaning in one's work, feeling engaged while at work, having a high-quality working life, and finding professional fulfillment in one's work (National Academies of Sciences, Engineering, and Medicine, 2019).

work-life balance

"Focuses on providing employees with greater flexibility in when, where, or how often they work, as well as benefits to assist them in managing nonwork demands" (Grawitch & Ballard, 2016).

References

Agency for Healthcare Research and Quality (AHRQ). (2013, May). Module 4. Approaches to Quality Improvement. In *Practice Facilitation Handbook*. https://www.ahrq.gov/ncepcr/tools/pf-handbook/mod4.html

Agency for Healthcare Research and Quality. (2014, June). Chapter 2. What Is Care Coordination? In *Care Coordination Measures Atlas Update*. https://www.ahrq.gov/ncepcr/care/coordination/atlas/chapter2.html

Agency for Healthcare Research and Quality. (2018, February). *Ambulatory Care*. https://www.ahrq.gov/patient-safety/settings/ambulatory/tools.html

Agency for Healthcare Research and Quality. (2020, March). Strategy 6P: Service Recovery Programs. In *The CAHPS Ambulatory Care Improvement Guide: Practical Strategies for Improving Patient Experience* (section 6). https://www.ahrq.gov/cahps/quality-improvement/improvement-guide/6-strategies-for-improving/customer-service/strategy6p-service-recovery.html

Agency for Healthcare Research and Quality. (2020, November). *AHRQ Quality Indicator Tools for Data Analytics*. https://www.ahrq.gov/data/qualityindicators/index.html

American Academy of Ambulatory Care Nursing. (n.d.). *Nurse-Sensitive Indicators*. Retrieved April 9, 2021, from https://www.aaacn.org/practice-resources/ambulatory-care/nurse-sensitive-indicators

American Association of Colleges of Nursing. (2006). *AACN Position Statement on Nursing Research*. Washington, DC: Author. https://www.aacnnursing.org/News-Information/Position-Statements-White-Papers/Nursing-Research

The American College of Obstetricians and Gynecologists. (2018, January). *Cultural sensitivity and awareness in the delivery of health care: Committee on Health Care for Underserved Women Opinion, Number 729*. ACOG.org. https://www.acog.org/clinical/clinical-guidance/committee-opinion/articles/2018/01/importance -of-social-determinants-of-health-and-cultural-awareness-in-the-delivery-of-reproductive-health-care

American Hospital Association. (2021, January). *Fast Facts on US Hospitals, 2021*. Retrieved March 29, 2021, from https://www.aha.org/statistics/fast-facts-us-hospitals

American Nurses Association. (1979). *The study of credentialing in nursing: A new approach* (Vol. I, report of the committee). Kansas City, MO: Author.

American Nurses Association. (1996). *Nursing quality indicators: Definitions and implications*. Washington, DC. Author

American Nurses Association. (2015a). *Code of ethics for nurses with interpretive statements*. Silver Spring, MD: Author.

American Nurses Association. (2015b). *Nursing: Scope and standards of practice* (3rd ed.). Silver Spring, MD: Author.

American Nurses Association. (2016). *Nursing administration: Scope and standards of practice* (2nd ed.). Silver Spring, MD. Author.

American Nurses Association. (2021). *Nursing: Scope and standards of practice* (4th ed.). Silver Spring, MD: Author.

American Nurses Association and National Nursing Staff Development Organization. (2010). *Nursing professional development: Scope and standards of practice*. Silver Spring, MD: Author.

American Nurses Credentialing Center. (2008). *Application manual: Magnet Recognition Program*. 2008. Silver Spring, MD: Author.

American Nurses Credentialing Center. (2013). *2014 Magnet® application manual*. Silver Spring, MD: Author.

American Nurses Credentialing Center. (2015). *Primary accreditation provider application manual.* Silver Spring, MD: Author.

American Nurses Credentialing Center. (2020). *2020 Application Manual: Practice Transition Accreditation Program® (PTAP)*. Silver Spring, MD: Author

Anthony, M. K. (2006). Professional Practice and Career Development. In D. L. Huber (Ed.), *Leadership and nursing care management* (3rd ed.; pp. 61–81). Philadelphia, PA: Saunders Elsevier.

Bamboo, H. R. (n.d.). *Performance review. An HR glossary for HR terms: Glossary of human resources management and employee benefit terms*. Retrieved April 11, 2021, from https://www.bamboohr.com/hr-glossary/performance-review/

Bartz, C. C. (2010). International council of nurses and person-centered care. *International Journal of Integrated Care, 10* (Sup), e010. https://doi.org/10.5334/ijic.480

Bass, B. M., & Riggio, R. E. (2006). *Transformational leadership* (2nd ed.). Mahwah, NJ: Lawrence Erlbaum Associates, Inc.

Benner, P., Tanner, C., & Chesla, C. (2009). *Expertise in nursing practice: Caring, clinical judgment, and ethics* (2nd ed). New York: Springer Publishing.

The Beryl Institute. (n.d.). *Patient Experience 101—Overview*. Retrieved April 11, 2021, from https://www.theberylinstitute.org/page/PX101

Bowen, C. (2020, February 12). *Patient Population*. Paubox. https://www.paubox.com/blog/patient-population

Burns, L. R., Bradley, E. H., & Weiner, B. L. (2012). *Shortell and Kaluzny's health care management: Organization, design, and behavior* (6th ed.). Clifton Park, NY: Delmar Cengage Learning.

Cain, C., & Haque, S. (2008). Organizational workflow and its impact on work quality. In R. G. Hughes (ed.), *Patient safety and quality: An evidence-based handbook for nurses* (AHRQ publication no. 08-0043) (ch. 31). Rockville, MD: Agency for Healthcare Research and Quality. Retrieved from https://archive.ahrq.gov/professionals/clinicians-providers/resources/nursing/resources/nurseshdbk/index.html

Curto, C., & Martin, D. (2020). The Magnet® site visit: Going virtual in response to COVID-19. *The Journal of Nursing Administration, 50*(11), 555–556.

D'amour, D., & Oandasan, I. (2005). Interprofessionality as the field of interprofessional practice and interprofessional education: An emerging concept. *Journal of interprofessional care, 19*(sup1), 8–20. https://doi.org/10.1080/13561820500081604

Darby, C., Valentine, N., De Silva, A., Murray, C. J., & World Health Organization. (2003). *World Health Organization (WHO): Strategy on measuring responsiveness*. https://apps.who.int/iris/handle/10665/68703

Dearholt, S. L., & Dang, D. (2012). *Johns Hopkins Nursing Evidence-Based Practice: Models and Guidelines* (2nd ed). Indianapolis, US: Sigma Theta Tau International.

Dempsey, C., & Reilly, B. (2016). Nurse engagement: What are the contributing factors for success? *OJIN: The Online Journal of Issues in Nursing, 21*(1), 2.

DePoy, E., & Gitlin, L. (2016). *Introduction to research: Understanding and applying multiple strategies* (5th ed.). St. Louis, MO: Elsevier.

Donabedian, A. (2003). *An introduction to quality assurance in health care*. New York: Oxford University Press.

Eggenberger, T., Sherman, R. O., & Keller, K. (2014). Creating high-performance interprofessional teams. *Am Nurse Today, 9*(11), 12–14.

Epstein, R. M., & Hundert, E. M. (2002). Defining and assessing professional competence. *JAMA, 287*(2), 226–235. https://doi.org/10.1001/jama.287.2.226

Farquharson, J. M. (2004). Liability of the Nurse Manager. In T. D. Aiken, *Legal, Ethical, and Political Issues in Nursing* (2nd ed.; pp. 311–336). Philadelphia, PA: F.A. Davis Company.

Frankel, A., Haraden, C., Federico, F., & Lenoci-Edwards, J. (2017). A framework for safe, reliable, and effective care. *White paper. Cambridge, MA: Institute for Healthcare Improvement and Safe & Reliable Healthcare.*

Friedman, J. P. (Ed.). (2012). *Barron's dictionary of business and economic terms* (5th ed.) Hauppauge, NY: Barron's Educational Series, Inc.

Gardner, D. B. (2005). Ten lessons in collaboration. *Online Journal of Issues in Nursing, 10*(1), 2.

Gourevitch, M. N. (2014). Population health and the academic medical center: The time is right. *Academic Medicine, 89*(4), 544–549.

Grawitch, M. J., & Ballard, D. W. (Eds.). (2016). *The psychologically healthy workplace: Building a win-win environment for organizations and employees*. American Psychological Association. https://doi.org/10.1037/14731-000

Griffith, J. R., & White, K. R. (2002). *The well-managed healthcare organization* (5th ed). Chicago: Health Administration Press.

Grossman, S. C., & Valiga, T. M. (2005). *The new leadership challenge: Creating the future of nursing* (2nd ed). Philadelphia: F.A. Davis Co.

Helmreich, R. L. (1998). Error management as organisational strategy. In *Proceedings of the IATA Human Factors Seminar* (pp. 1–7). Bangkok, Thailand, April 20–22, 1998.

Indeed. (2020, December 27). *Q&A: What is a professional organization?*. Indeed Career Guide. https://www.indeed.com/career-advice/career-development/what-is-a-professional-organization

Institute for Credentialing Excellence. (2020). *Basic guide to credentialing terminology* (2nd ed). Institute for Credentialing Excellence. https://www.credentialingexcellence.org/

Institute of Medicine. (2000). *To err is human: Building a safety health system*. (Kohn, L. T., Corrigan, J. M., & Donaldson, M. S., Eds.). National Academies Press (US). https://doi.org/10.17226/9728

Institute of Medicine. (2001a). *Crossing the quality chasm: A new health system for the 21st century*. The National Academies Press (US). https://doi.org/10.17226/10027

Institute of Medicine. (2001b). *Envisioning the national health care quality report*. National Academy Press. https://doi.org/10.17226/10073

Institute of Medicine. (2004). *Patient safety: Achieving a new standard for care*. (Aspden, P., Corrigan, J. M., Wolcott, J., & Erickson, S. M., Eds.). National Academies Press (US). https://doi.org/10.17226/10863

Institute of Medicine. (2011). *The future of nursing: Leading change, advancing health*. National Academies Press (US).

The Joint Commission. (2017). Patient Safety Systems (PS). In *Comprehensive accreditation manual for hospitals* (pp. PS1-PS50). Oak Brook, IL: Joint Commission Resources. Retrieved from https://www.jointcommission.org/patient_safety_systems_chapter_for_the_hospital_program

Kaya, N., Turan, N., & Aydin, G. O. (2015). A concept analysis of innovation in nursing. *Procedia—Social and Behavioral Sciences, 195*, 1674–1678.

Kindig, D., & Stoddart, G. (2003). What Is Population Health? *American Journal of Public Health, 93*, 380–383.

Lake, E. T. (2002). Development of the practice environment scale of the nursing work index. *Research in Nursing & Health, 25*(3), 176–188.

Laughlin, C. B., & Witwer, S. G. (Eds.). (2019). *Core curriculum for ambulatory care nursing* (4th ed.). Pitman, NJ: American Academy of Ambulatory Care Nursing.

Magnet hospitals. Attraction and retention of professional nurses. Task Force on Nursing Practice in Hospitals. American Academy of Nursing. (1983). *American Nurses Association Publications, G-160*, i–xiv, 1–135.

Malloch, K., & Porter-O'Grady, T. (2010). *Introduction to evidence-based practice in nursing and health care*. Burlington, Massachusetts: Jones and Bartlett Learning.

Merriam-Webster. (n.d.). *Merriam-Webster.com dictionary*. Retrieved March 29, 2021, from https://www.merriam-webster.com/dictionary

Mosby. (2017). *Mosby's dictionary of medicine, nursing and health professions* (10th ed.). Cambridge, MA: Elsevier.

National Academies of Sciences, Engineering, and Medicine. (2019). *Taking action against clinician burnout: A systems approach to professional well-being*. Washington, DC: National Academies Press.

National Advisory Council on Nurse Education and Practice. (2013). *Achieving health equity through nursing workforce diversity*. https://www.hrsa.gov/sites/default/files/hrsa/advisory-committees/nursing/reports/2013-eleventhreport.pdf

National Institute for Occupational Safety and Health. (2020, September 22). *Occupational Violence*. https://www.cdc.gov/niosh/topics/violence/default.html

National Prevention Information Network. (2020, October 21). *Cultural competence in health and human services*. https://npin.cdc.gov/pages/cultural-competence

National Quality Forum. (2004). *National voluntary consensus standards for nursing-sensitive care: An initial performance measure set*. Washington, DC: National Quality Forum.

NEJM Catalyst. (2017). What is patient-centered care? *NEJM Catalyst Innovations in Care Delivery, 3*(1). https://catalyst.nejm.org/doi/full/10.1056/CAT.17.0559

Polit, D. (2010). *Statistics and Data Analysis for Nursing Research* (2nd ed.). Saratoga Springs, NY: Pearson.

Polit, D. F., & Beck, C. T. (2017). *Nursing research: Generating and assessing evidence for nursing practice* (10th ed.). Philadelphia: Wolters Kluwer Health.

Pollard, P. B., Andres, N. K., & Dobson, A. (1996). *Nursing quality indicators: Definitions and implications*. American Nurses Association.

Shortell, S. M., & Kaluzny, A. D. (2006). *Health care management: Organization design and behavior* (5th ed.). Clifton Park, NY: Thomson Delmar Learning.

Silverstein, W., & Kowalski, M. O. (2017). Adapting a professional practice model. *American Nurse Today, 12*(9), 78–83. https://www.myditialpublication.com/publication/?m=41491&i=435651&p=84&ver=html5

Titzer, J. L., & Shirey, M. R. (2013). Nurse manager succession planning: A concept analysis. *Nursing Forum, 48* (33), 155–164.

Vanderbilt University Medical Center. (n.d.). *Shared governance*. Retrieved April 11, 2021, from https://www.vumc.org/shared-governance/welcome

von Eiff, W. (2015). International benchmarking and best practice management: In search of health care and hospital excellence. *International Best Practices in Health Care Management,* 17, 223–252. https://doi.org/10.1108/S1474-823120140000017014

Weston, M. (2010). Strategies for Enhancing Autonomy and Control Over Nursing Practice. *Online Journal of Issues in Nursing, 15*(1). https://doi.org/10.3912/OJIN.Vol15No01Man02

Witmer, A., Seifer, S. D., Finocchio, L., Leslie, J., & O'Neil, E. H. (1995). Community health workers: Integral members of the health care work force. *American Journal of Public Health, 85*(8), Pt 1: 1055–1058.

World Health Organization. (2010). *Framework for action on interprofessional education and collaborative practice*. Geneva, Switzerland: Author. http://www.who.int/hrh/resources/framework_action/en/

World Health Organization. (2016, August 20). *Health promotion*. https://www.who.int/news-room/q-a-detail/health-promotion